I BEGIN WITH
SPRING

The Life and Seasons
of Henry David Thoreau

Written by
Julie Dunlap

Illustrated by
Megan Elizabeth Baratta

TILBURY HOUSE PUBLISHERS

white oak
acorns

Why do the seasons change?

white pine

winter

yellow warbler

spring

white oak, autumn

swamp
milkweed,
summer

These words begin the earliest existing writing of Henry David Thoreau, in a school report composed at age 11 or 12, called "The Seasons." Nature and its endless cycles already fascinated the boy, born in Concord, Massachusetts, in 1817. By observing and recording when flowers bloom, birds nest and migrate, and leaves appear and turn colors, Henry would change how we understand the shifting seasons and our place in the natural world.

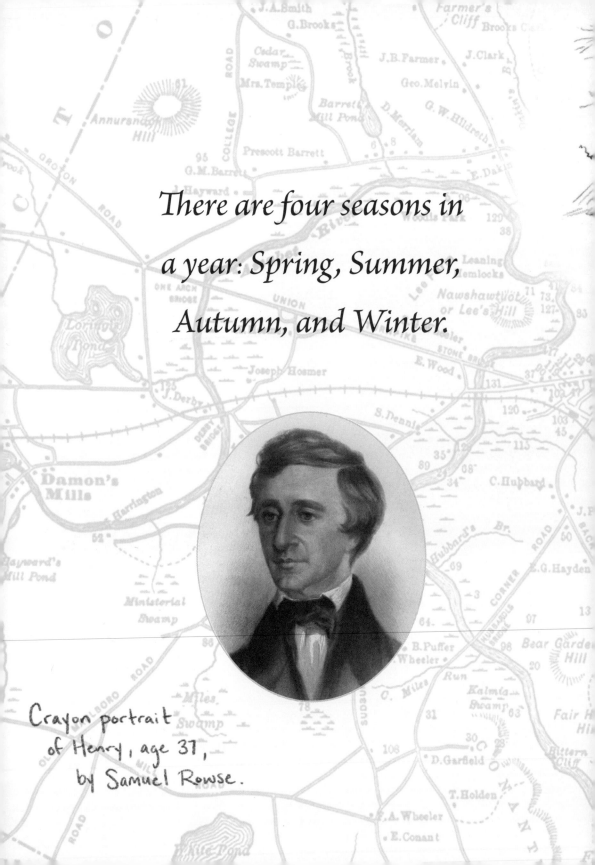

There are four seasons in a year: Spring, Summer, Autumn, and Winter.

Crayon portrait of Henry, age 37, by Samuel Rowse.

Henry was born in this farmhouse on Virginia Road in Concord.

I will begin with Spring.

Young Henry could follow his nose to the first flower blooms each year. Born on his grandmother's farm, the third of four children, from his earliest springs he rambled the boggy woods in search of skunk cabbage.

March 2	March 4	March 6	March 8
Last snow buntings?	Winds gusty	Black birch catkins out	Snow melt shows skunk cabbage buds

skunk cabbage

On hands and knees through slushy snow, Henry
crept close to the hooded blossoms—close enough
to hear a fly buzz inside.

Someday he would know the woods so well, he'd find wild
cherries and water lilies by their scents too. But the
rotten-meat stink of skunk cabbage would always
lift his winter-worn spirits.

March 17	March 20	March 21
Heavy thunder showers	Tapped birch sap	Earliest alder bloom

Spathe:
leaf that acts
like a hood.

Spadix:
tiny flowers
(nibbled by mouse?)

When other flowers still hide below
ground, skunk cabbages in March
shoot toward the sky.

striped
skunk

Henry thought
he knew why:
"They see another
summer ahead."

March 23	March 26	March 28
Two hen-hawks; could not find nest	First croaking frogs; geese at Walden	Soil thawed enough for planting

Now we see the ice beginning to thaw, and the trees to bud.

As a boy, Henry preferred finding wildflowers to plucking them. Later he tucked blossoms, leaves, and seeds in a "botany hat" to observe at home, too.

Years after Henry died, his sister Sophia inscribed his poem "Fair Haven" on leaves.

An unknown plant could be checked in books and under a magnifying lens. Pressed, dried, and pasted onto a sheet of paper, it became a study specimen. In the 1850s, he added scientific names (in Latin) to each record. Stacks of pressings added up year after year, building Henry's herbarium, a personal museum of over 900 specimens.

His sister Sophia turned her collection into art. She inscribed a poem of Henry's onto a hickory leaf, and decorated a checkerboard with pressed ferns. Sister and brother often raced each other for favorite spring blooms.

Henry mailed his best specimens to a Harvard professor, Louis Agassiz. A famed biologist and geologist, Agassiz invited the public to send their finds to the college museum because many of North America's plants and animals still needed to be formally identified and described.

Once Henry packed up three boxes of fish and a turtle from Concord's Walden Pond, plus a letter crammed with questions. Professor Agassiz's reply was thrilling—please send more! "Nature will bear the closest inspection," said Henry.

April 1	April 2	April 5	April 6
Gloves only in morning	Bluebirds, robins singing	Mizzling rain	8 inches of snow

Now the Winter
wears away, and the ground
begins to look green with
the new born grass.

Botany, algebra, Greek, and writing lessons at the Concord Academy kept Henry inside the year he turned 11. Students tried to sit stiff in their chairs to avoid a caning. When the doors finally opened, everyone rushed out with a whoop!

But Henry watched the others' games from a fence rail. One called him "an odd stick," and many preferred John, the easygoing Thoreau brother, to shy Henry.

Few knew how loud John and Henry laughed and sang on spring Saturdays in the new-leafed woods. They tramped all day, collecting stones and hunting arrowheads in blustery April storms.

Their mother never fussed when the boys returned mud-soaked and dripping.

"To see wild life," Henry later said, "you must go forth at a wild season."

The free-roaming boys in the 1820s did not know their woods and fields had once looked very, very different.

But in the 1830s Professor Agassiz lived in Switzerland and began to study slow-moving rivers of ice called glaciers.

Prof. Agassiz

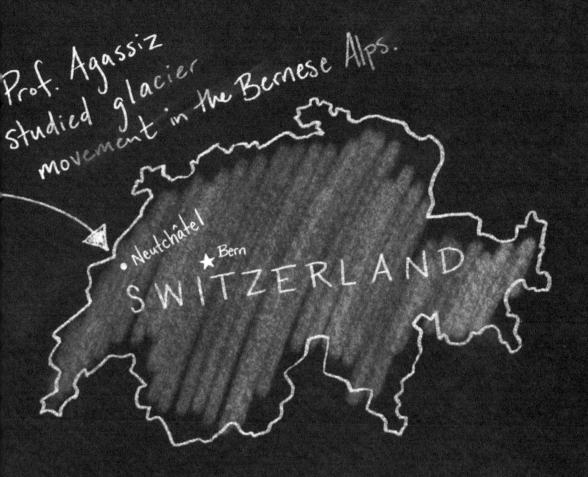

Prof. Agassiz studied glacier movement in the Bernese Alps.

• Neutchâtel
★ Bern

SWITZERLAND

The evidence told him that Earth had been much colder in the past. New England geologists read his theory and found similar evidence in their own hills and ponds. Mile-thick ice sheets had shaped and scarred their landscape too, retreating as the climate warmed about 15,000 years ago.

April 16 | April 17 | April 18

First bank swallow | Willow catkins | Dandelion open, will shed pollen tomorrow

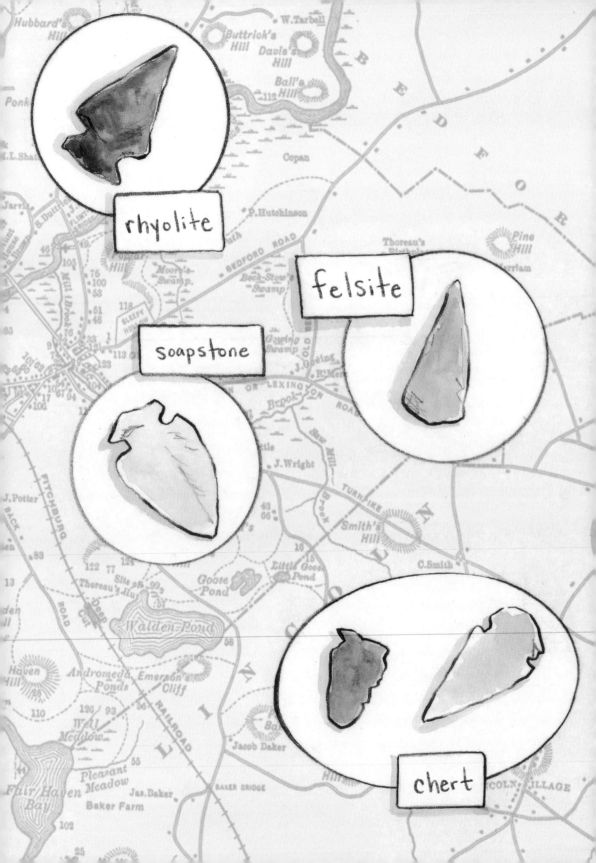

rhyolite

felsite

soapstone

chert

Arrowheads told Henry other stories
about the past. They were made from
different kinds of stone, depending
on how their makers used them.
The places he found stone knives and
pot shards told him that ancient
peoples hunted and
camped in rich forests
where his neighbors
now farmed.

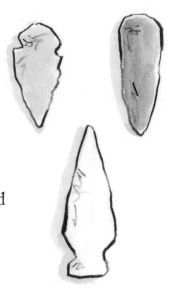

When Henry found an
arrowhead and fingered the
still-sharp edge, the maker
came alive to him.

Thawing soil made spring
the best time to find "stone
fruit," he said. "Each one
yields me a thought."

April 25	April 30	May 1	May 3
...een starting to prevail; first wood thrush	Horse chestnut leafing	Birdsfoot violet blooms	Sit without fire

The birds which have lately been to more southern countries return again to cheer us with their morning song.

Sweet; Sweet; Sweet; little-more-Sweet

Yellow Warbler ("yellowbird")

The adventurous brothers also knew how to be quiet.

Standing still in a thicket, John cupped a hand behind each ear, showing Henry how to hear the faintest birdsong. Those melodies announced that warblers absent all winter were back again to nest.

yellow warbler nest with eggs

When Henry turned 15, they built a rowboat to explore Concord's rivers and ponds. The Thoreaus floated and dreamed of Algonquin boys who had fished the same waters, of moose and lynx that once stepped among the pines.

Without those people and wild creatures, the shadowed forest sometimes felt lonely. It was as if someone had torn out pages from a great book. "I should not like to think," Henry later wrote, "some demigod had come before me and picked out some of the best of the stars."

May 7	May 8	May 9	May 10
First yellowbirds when willows leaf out	Gold robins in town elms	Planted melons; highbush blueberry blooms	Low notes of bullfrog, "kerdle dont dont"

American goldfinch

While rowing streams and ponds
and hiking woods and wetlands, the
brothers learned the voices of birds,
frogs, and insects too.

Song
Sparrow

Maids-Maids-Maids-
put-on-your-tea-Kettle-
ettle-ettle

patect-patect-patect

Spring field cricket

If they didn't recognize a song,
they might lie on the ground for
hours to spot the singer.

clack
clack
clack

Wood frog

belted kingfisher

Wood thrush

Northern parula

The spring jumble
of chirps and warbles
grated on some ears;
townsfolk wanted to keep their minds
on business. But Henry heard "a night-warbler,
wood thrush, kingfisher, tweezer-bird or
particolored warbler, and a nighthawk."
How could he feel lonesome
for long, surrounded by
such tuneful neighbors?

ovenbird
(Thoreau's "night-warbler"?)

nighthawk
in flight

WALDEN POND

The map Henry created
while living at Walden.

A drafting instrument
used to draw
precise maps.

The family could afford to send only one son to college, and they chose more-studious Henry. On breaks from Latin, German, and history classes, he hunted bird nests in farmland near Boston, but missed Concord's countryside.

The library was his favorite spot at Harvard. Books held knowledge never taught in his classrooms, like the Wampanoag language spoken by Concord's indigenous people.

And math courses built skills that would help solve a Concord mystery. Some believed that deep, clear Walden Pond was bottomless.

May 14	May 15	May 21	May 22
Black-billed cuckoo catching caterpillars	Warblers hunting insects in trees	White oak leaves and catkins	Town smells of lilacs

paper birch
flowers, or
catkins

One winter,
Henry ventured
onto the ice with
a sounding line,
weighted with stone, to
measure the truth: 102 feet
at the deepest. "It is remarkable how long
men will believe in the bottomlessness of a
pond without taking the trouble to sound it."

Some Saturdays, homesick Henry might
walk the 20 miles home to Concord. The
closer he looked at the life around him, the
better he saw that seasons overlap and flow
into each other. Early spring blooms
fade as new flowers unfold,
and early summer buds
mix with spring's
final blossoms.

lilac
early spring
May 5

Each day to him became
almost its own season. He said,
"Hardly two nights are alike."

May 23

May 25

Wade into swamp for
kalmia (bog laurel)

Found five
arrowheads

New England cottontail

(late bloom –
June 10)

birdsfoot violet
Viola pedata

Next comes Summer.

Wild strawberries
Fragaria virginiana

rry Pie

highbush
blueberries
(Vaccinium corymbosum)

May
20th

(picking party
in late July!)

bloom
time
late August–
early Sept.

garden
sunflower

The first issue of *The Dial*, which Emerson called "a Journal in a new spirit," included Henry's first published writing.

THE DIAL:

A

MAGAZINE

FOR

LITERATURE, PHILOSOPHY, AND RELIGION.

TO BE CONTINUED QUARTERLY.

No. I.

JULY, 1840.

BOSTON:
WEEKS, JORDAN, AND COMPANY,
121 WASHINGTON STREET.
LONDON:
WILEY AND PUTNAM, 67 PATERNOSTER ROW.
M DCCC XL.

CAMBRIDGE PRESS: — METCALF, TORRY, AND BALLOU.

Lysimachia terrestris

Swamp candles
(aka upright loosestrife)

spring azure

Celastrina ladon

(Habitat: Openings and edges of deciduous woods, old fields, wooded freshwater marshes and swamps.)

After Henry finished college, the brothers opened their own school. Girls and boys learned geography by drawing maps, botany by planting melons, and math by surveying the cliffs at Fairhaven Pond on Concord's Sudbury River. History lived when the 21-year-old teacher plunged a shovel into river mud--unearthing fire-marked rocks from an Algonquian fishing camp.

Tragically, John fell ill and died in 1842. Henry lost his best friend.

With the school closed, how could he make a living? He tried odd jobs like helping farmers build fences and pick peas. For the family's pencil company, he invented a machine to mill graphite for a harder, blacker lead, and the business boomed.

But Henry longed to be a writer, a poet. A writer-friend, Ralph Waldo Emerson, had urged him to start a journal, and Henry crafted those raw thoughts into essays and poems. His pride swelled when a new publication, *The Dial*, printed a few. But it paid nothing.

Without John, words kept him company on summer walks along a shady riverbank. Some in town sniffed, Shouldn't that Thoreau boy start making some money? But Henry told his journal, "Where the most beautiful wild flowers grow—there Man's spirit is fed—& poets grow—"

June 5	June 6	June 8	June 10
Woodpecker nest in apple tree	Sphinx moth on honeysuckles in evening	White pine in flower	First sleep with open window

J. Thoreau & Son pencils became the best in the country. Engineers and accountants replaced messy quill pens with sharp-pointed pencils. Carpenters bought flat ones designed not to roll away, and artists could draw violets with a new blue color. More experiments showed Henry how to make leads that marked softer or harder for different uses. But powdered graphite hung thick in the factory air, and soot from the wood-burning stoves scratched at his lungs.

apple blossom

June 11
Heard night warbler?

June 13
To Walden
in moonlight

June 14
4 eggs in meadow
peetweet nest

Baltimore oriole
(gold robin)

black
cherry
blossoms

Outdoors, he could breathe
deeply. His pencils wrote well
in summer sun or any season.

J. THOREAU & SON

J. THOREAU & SON

June 15

Suddenly hot

June 16

Scent of
waterlilies

June 21

Yellowbird nest
in willows

Mt. Monadnock — 3166'

42.8611° N , 72.1083° W

After losing John, Henry turned to friends as travel companions.

One August, Henry camped with poet-friend Ellery Channing on New Hampshire's Mount Monadnock. Cool under the stars, the men listened to nighthawks.

Only Henry rose before dawn and breakfasted on cranberries. He took notes for days on the mountain's plants, birds, and insects, and sketched lines carved in the stones by long-lost glaciers.

"We cannot see anything," Henry wrote, "until we are possessed with the idea of it, take it into our heads—and then we can hardly see anything else."

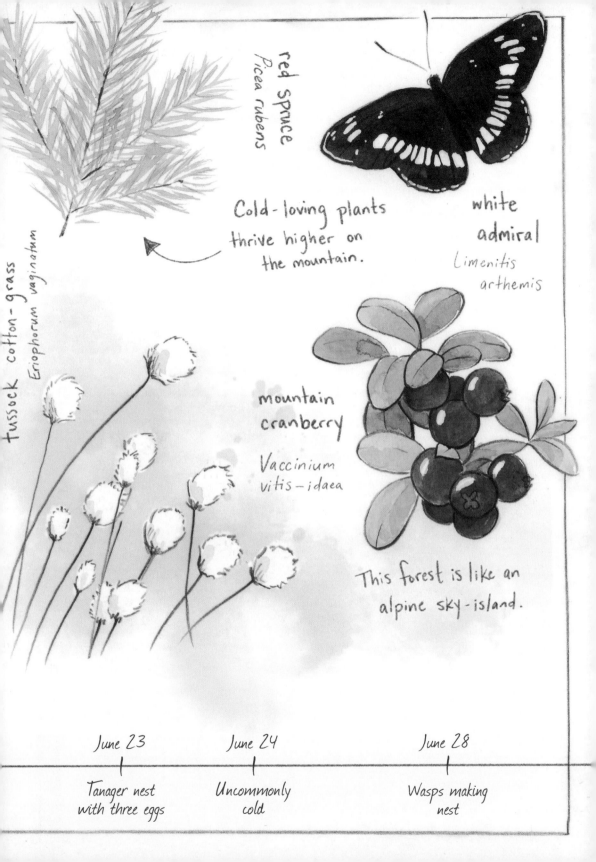

red spruce
Picea rubens

white
admiral
*Limenitis
arthemis*

Cold-loving plants
thrive higher on
the mountain.

tussock cotton-grass
Eriophorum vaginatum

mountain
cranberry

*Vaccinium
vitis-idaea*

This forest is like an
alpine sky-island.

June 23
Tanager nest
with three eggs

June 24
Uncommonly
cold

June 28
Wasps making
nest

The trees and flowers are in bloom.

Unsure what job to try next, Henry decided to experiment with his own life. By living more simply, could he have more time for his real work: writing?

Emerson offered space in a woodlot, and Henry borrowed an ax to chop a few pine trees. Emerson, Bronson Alcott, and other friends helped raise a wood frame and nailed on boards repurposed from an old hut.

Henry's house by Sophia Thoreau

The tiny house, with a bed, a desk, and three chairs, cost $28.12 ½. That was enough for Henry.

great horned owl

July 4, 1845, was Henry's Independence Day. He moved to Walden Pond. A hooting owl kept him company at night.

Mornings began with a dip in the pond. Then there were wildflowers to find, beans to hoe—and a woodchuck to battle over who would eat the crop.

On a hot afternoon, Henry lay silent in the shade of a locust tree and let animals come to him. A bold mouse nibbled cheese from his fingers, and the heat ripened his ideas along with the huckleberries.

mountain laurel

"I was rich," he later wrote, "if not in money, in sunny hours and summer days. . . and I spent them lavishly."

Agassiz says white-bellied mouse

Sometimes, Henry welcomed visitors
by placing a chair outside his door.

Family came often to picnic by the
water, or 12-year-old Louisa May
Alcott and her sisters, Bronson's
daughters, visited to pick huckleberries
and glide in Henry's boat, watching
the high clouds roll by.

huckleberry
Gaylussacia baccata

But the peace was broken daily
with shrieks of a train whistle.
Built to speed more goods and
people around Massachusetts,
the rail line was just finished in
1845. Locomotives now belched
black smoke from burning
Concord's pitch pines into
Walden's blue sky.

July 3

Ovenbird nest
under oak leaves

July 5

Water milkweed
blooming

A friend urged Henry to earn cash to buy a ticket. Henry
thought of all he would miss on a summer's day on the rails.
"I am wiser than that," he said, and cleaned his boots.

July 3–7
Earliest ripe
highbush blueberries

July 7
Fog,
bird song

July 12
Henry's
birthday!

The pond was also the perfect spot to talk with friends about transcendentalism, a philosophy many shared, that nature holds answers to our most profound questions.

yellow perch

Scientific name: Perca flavecens

Phylum: Chordata

Emerson said often that solitude outdoors teaches people how to think for themselves.

July 15 — Butterflies on water milkweed

July 16 — Bluebird song sounds like spring

July 20 — Polliwags turned into frogs

His heart was kind and soft, · · Faith - ful be - low he

did his du - ty, And now he's gone a - loft, · · And now he's gone a - loft.

More radical transcendentalists wanted a revolution. They believed society should focus on spiritual needs, not material things. Bronson Alcott started a community called Fruitlands, where members refused cotton clothing because no one should profit from the labor of slaves.

Henry thought about these ideas long after his friends went home. Floating on the pond, he played his brother's favorite song, and perch gathered around the boat, charmed by his flute.

The letters "JT" are inscribed on the ivory end cap.

Now the fruit begins to form on the trees, and all things look beautiful.

blackberries
Rubus pensylvanicus

Henry often walked two miles into town to run errands or help with pencil-making. Neighbors might follow him home to Walden, eager to be shown the sweetest blackberry patches.

Along the way, they peppered Henry with questions. Why did you move to the woods? Why live alone? Will your writing—your art!—suffer if you study nature too closely?

July 24
Hot, blackberries
abundant

July 29
Butterflies on
early goldenrod

August 2
Zzzzz of
locust in grass

Young crows have fledged!

American crow

Corvus brachyrhynchos

Henry's reply was to whistle a crow down from the trees. He knew: "The question is not what you look at, but what you see."

August 4	August 6	August 9
Swallows – ready to migrate?	Haymakers in meadows	Goldfinch nest with five eggs

As Henry hoped, simple living at Walden brought more writing time. Before the evening light faded, he transferred field notes into his journal, recording pond water temperature, the number of passing geese, and stream depth after a rain.

common loon

Gavia immer

And he told of rowing after a loon, keen to see it closer. The bird dove down and popped up, over and over, tricking Henry to keep chasing. The game ended with Henry's arms aching and the loon's wild laugh "making the woods ring."

August 13	August 14	August 15
Pewee nests now empty	Great blue heron fishing in river	Flock of bobolinks

The story that meant most was a memory. In his little house, with the scent of pine drifting in his window, a boat trip with John to the White Mountains lived again on paper. He wove together misty mornings and steamy afternoons on the water with lofty thoughts on beauty, religion, river commerce, loss, and timeless love.

The story became Henry's first book, *A Week on the Concord and Merrimack River*, a lasting tribute to his brother.

Henry's desk

August 17
|
Smell of
apples ripening

August 20
|
Hunting crickets
to learn songs

Henry savored his liberty to write and think at Walden for 2 years, 2 months, and 2 days. In fact, the Walden experiment proved to him that freedom is one of life's necessities.

But he could not forget America's greatest injustice in the 1840s: slavery. Black people bound by legal chains had no freedom at all.

In protest, he refused for years to pay a tax. In his view, the money backed a U.S. war with Mexico that expanded slavery to Texas. In July 1846, on an errand to the town cobbler, he was stopped by the sheriff. Sam Staples gave Henry a choice: pay his back taxes or go to jail. He chose jail.

Anti-slavery friends and family applauded, but others called the action "silly" and in "bad taste." Without Henry's permission, someone secretly paid the money to get him released.

goldenrod
Solidago sp.

front

back

1846
U.S. silver
dollar

1846

UNITED STATES of AMERICA

ONE DOL.

Henry relied on his own
judgment, recognizing a
duty to resist a law that
is morally wrong. He
declared, "Let your life
be a counter-friction to
stop the machine."

August 21
Yellow spider
on goldenrod

August 22
Pottery found
after heavy rain

August 23
Pokeweed
stems purple

In Autumn
we see the
trees loaded
with fruit.

Now the farmers begin
to lay their Winter's
store, and the markets
abound with fruit.

apple
pie !

After two years, Henry left Walden Pond to test other ways of living.

Unsold copies of his first book stacked up in his parents' attic. "I have now a library of nearly 900 volumes," Henry joked, "over 700 of which I wrote myself."

But locked in his desk were notes for a new book about life in the woods. He felt a new excitement outdoors too. The first book about New England botany, published in 1848, sparked a fresh intensity in his plant studies. He walked at least four hours a day in fall, with asters and goldenrod tucked in his botany hat.

August 25

Paddled meadows
after river flood

August 29

Heard eagle
scream in clouds

August 31

Few birds
except crows

Instead of packing lunch, he snatched wild fruit to quiet his stomach. If eaten by his desk, the first fall apples tasted sour enough to "make a jay scream." But on a brisk hike, they were spicy and sweet. Henry said wild apples should be labeled: "To be eaten in the wind."

milkweed seeds

Fall seeds especially
mesmerized Henry.

Gray squirrel

Thistle seeds brought
goldfinches down
from the trees, and
squirrels buried
acorns that would
grow a new forest.

Seed studies made him question scientists, like
Agassiz, who said plant and animal species never
change, and exist on Earth wherever placed at
first Creation. Henry wondered: why would maple
seeds have wings if not to travel on the breeze?

Early September	September 4	September 6
Passenger pigeons eating acorns	Grasshoppers flying	Scent of ripening grapes

When he found a milkweed pod, he knew
flat brown seeds grew inside, each with its
own silk parachute. Cracked open, the pod
released hundreds of seeds into the air, higher
and higher, toward a chance at life next year.
Milkweed devote their summers to making seeds,
Henry said, perfecting "a prophesy . . . of future springs."

milkweed pods
Asclepias sp.

September 9
Collecting white
pine cones

September 11
Frost in
low ground

On September 30, 1851, a foot-sore man arrived on the Thoreau doorstep. Henry Williams had escaped from slavery in Virginia to live in Boston, where slave-holding had been illegal since 1783.

CAUTION!!

COLORED PEOPLE

OF BOSTON, ONE & ALL,

You are hereby respectfully CAUTIONED and advised, to avoid conversing with the

Watchmen and Police Officers of Boston,

For since the recent ORDER OF THE MAYOR & ALDERMEN, they are empowered to act as

KIDNAPPERS

AND

Slave Catchers,

And they have already been actually employed in KIDNAPPING, CATCHING, AND KEEPING SLAVES. Therefore, if you value your LIBERTY, and the *Welfare of the Fugitives* among you, *Shun* them in every possible manner, as so many *HOUNDS* on the track of the most unfortunate of your race.

Keep a Sharp Look Out for KIDNAPPERS, and have TOP EYE open.

APRIL 24, 1851.

Sophia Thoreau

But a slave-catcher was on his trail. The 1850 U.S. Fugitive Slate Law required the man's return to his legal owner, so Mr. Williams had fled again, to an Underground Railroad station at the Thoreau house in Concord.

The family sheltered their guest while raising funds for a train ticket to Canada.

September 15

Many passenger pigeons

September 20

Hard frost kills melons, last crickets

September 22

First red maple leaves turn crimson

Helen, Henry's sister

Asked how he found his way, Mr.
Williams said he followed the stars
and telegraph lines north to freedom.

In the morning, Henry risked more time
in jail driving Mr. Williams to the train.
In a season when wild geese journeyed
south, a black man flew north
to escape his own
government.

Canada geese flying South

Inflamed, Henry wrote,
"My thoughts are murder to the State, and
involuntarily go plotting against her."

September 28	October 1		October 5
Frost ripens persimmons	First wear winter coat		Blackbirds leave when frost kills insects

The trees are partly stripped of their leaves.

October brought the finest days of Henry's year. Clean cold air refreshed his lungs, and his stride lengthened over crunching leaves.

leaf

Notes in the 1850s recorded the precise day when maple trees on different hills turned crimson, and celebrated the "thousand hues" of oaks, maples, chestnuts, and birches.

sugar maple —
in autumn the leaves
turn deep red,
orange, and yellow.

samaras
(seed)

white birch leaves and seeds

To make the most of every outing, Henry carried a notebook and pencil, jackknife, twine, hand lens, and an old music book for pressing samples.

Farmers gladly greeted Henry when he walked by. Was he sorry for another summer gone, fallen in leaves at his feet? To Henry, brown leaves were reminders of ceaseless natural cycles, life renewing life. "We are all the richer for their decay."

ouch

(Most American chestnuts around Concord had been cut for wood in Henry's time. Later, a disease killed the rest.)

horse chestnut leaves + fruit

Critics admired *Walden; or,
Life in the Woods*, when it
was published in 1854. One
called it "a brave book,"
another "a fresh bouquet from
the wilds." Sales were modest,
though, and writing still did
not pay Henry's bills.

This time he took up a trade:
land surveying. With a
compass and chain, he
measured out farm fields
and woodlots, roads and
fence lines. Precise work earned him respect around
town—neighbors arguing over boundaries used
Henry's maps to settle their disputes.

Plan of A. B. Alcott's estate
by Henry

October 7

Fall leaves reflect
in Walden ripples

October 9

Witch hazel blooms
smell like spring

October 11

Jays eating
ripe chestnuts

engineer chain

And he learned more about the curves and
angles of the land, the chilly damp hollows
where winter arrives first, and the sunny
hillsides where spring returns early.

But it caught in Henry's throat that
his work helped tame the countryside.
Places he had
    seen,
        heard,
            smelled,
    and tasted in every season
    became lines on paper, drawn
        to the quarter inch.

Aimless wandering taught him more.
"Not till we are lost," Henry wrote,
"do we begin to find ourselves. . . ."

Eastern-tailed
blue butterfly

Spotted while
surveying
Marlborough
Road

October 14
|
Black duck on
White Pond

October 15
|
Ice on
ponds

Living at home, Henry tasted the fall harvest daily in his mother's cooking. Talk was always lively, though with boarders at the table the Thoreaus kept silent about Underground Railroad work. After dinner, Henry might heat popcorn over the fire as a treat for everyone.

Even in chilly October, sugar maples on Concord's streets glowed with stored summer light. Henry thought autumn leaves would be better than a paintbox for teaching children colors.

In his journal, he thanked the town founders for keeping some space for trees. On the square, even the poorest children could feast their eyes on fall's bounty. Every town should have a leafy park, he thought. "All children alike can revel in this golden harvest."

"Central Part of Concord, Mass. "

drawn by J.W. Barber
engraved by J.D. Worcester

October 16
|
Fingers cold
when rowing

October 17
|
Found chestnut
seedlings under pines

October 22
|
Frost unlocks
chestnut burrs

Ovenbird
Seivrus aurocapilla

Like other writers, Henry spent long hours at his desk. When he wasn't writing, he read and re-read favorite books like Charles Darwin's *The Voyage of the Beagle*.

blue - and - yellow macaw
Ara ararauna

On board for Darwin's five-year expedition had been his favorite writing by an earlier explorer-scientist, Alexander von Humboldt. Henry loved Humboldt's work too, especially the multi-volume *Kosmos*.

why here?

October 24 | October 26 | October 27
Highbush blueberry leaves scarlet | Rain ends in snow | Woodcock feeding in mud

All of Humboldt's adventures—from South American rainforests to the Russian steppes—sought to discover how the complex world is ordered to work in harmony. *Kosmos* was his written attempt, Humboldt said, to find "unity in diversity."

Henry's quest in the 1850s was becoming more like Humboldt's. His hours afoot sought to determine why oaks and ovenbirds lived in Concord, not palm trees and parrots. Every day he asked, "Why do precisely these objects which we behold make a world?"

October 29	October 31	November 1
Jay gathering acorns	Skunk cabbage still green	Rowed by muskrat cabin

The birds which visited us in Spring are now retiring to warmer countries, as they know that Winter is coming.

For years, Henry resisted using a spyglass to magnify his view. He wanted to see with his own unaltered senses. But in 1854, he bought a glass for watching birds.

Henry's spyglass

November 6	November 8	November 9
Woods almost leafless	First snow	Found two arrowheads in rye field

Young Henry had shot birds to study them; now he trained his scope on the sky. With a glass, he could watch for the first winter finches after the last yellow warblers disappeared for the year.

Bird watching with spyglass!

Pine grosbeak — *Pinicola enucleator*

olor palette

Henry had begun to question some practices of scientific examination. Does a dead *Perca flavescens*, floating in alcohol, reveal as much as a live perch in Walden Pond?

The spyglass helped him reach closer to his goals as a writer and naturalist, to learn about birds in their own element. "I wanted to know my neighbors if possible—to get a little nearer to them."

November 10	November 13	November 14
Hear jays hammering acorns	Trees leafless, No insects hum	Cutting wind rustles leaves

Everywhere he went, the scope offered a new perspective.

After one early frost, he donned a greatcoat and climbed a hill to look down on Walden Pond. To his surprise, a thin film of ice had formed in the night. The first of the year.

"There is just as much beauty visible to us in the landscape as we are prepared to appreciate—not a grain more."

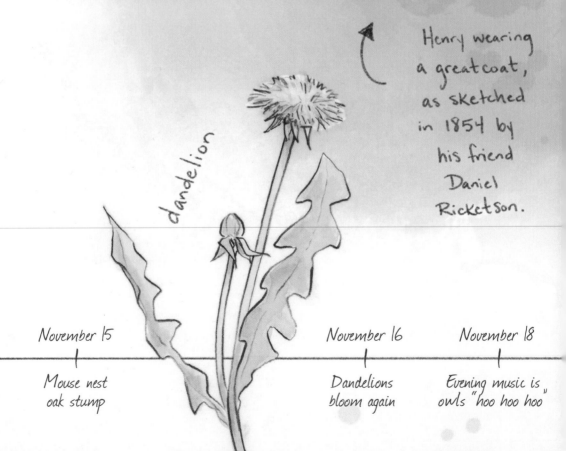

Henry wearing a greatcoat, as sketched in 1854 by his friend Daniel Ricketson.

dandelion

November 15
|
Mouse nest
oak stump

November 16
|
Dandelions
bloom again

November 18
|
Evening music is
owls "hoo hoo hoo"

passenger pigeon
Ectopistes migratorius

(extinct since 1914,
shot for meat
and sport.)

American chestnut stump ✳

✳ Nuts
from
American
chestnuts
once fed
vast flocks
of
passenger
pigeons.

November 21	November 22	November 23
Fish hawks sail over Fair Haven Pond	Only apples to eat on walk	Sixth geese flock heading south this week

With the spyglass in his knapsack, Henry set out in 1857 on his wildest adventure. Henry and his friend Edward Hoar traveled by train to explore the Maine woods. They were guided by a Penobscot elder, Joseph Polis. In a birchbark canoe crafted by Polis, the men slipped past fir-scented islands and careened over rocky rapids. Shallow passages required hauling gear through cold, knee-deep mud, testing the trio's toughness.

November 24
Warm sunny places, plucked a buttercup

November 25
Cutting wind, frozen ground

Warming up by the evening campfire, Henry and Edward listened to Joseph's stories of the forest where he lived in every season. Hearing Penobscot names for animals and unimagined uses for plants reminded Henry of how much he still had to learn.

Joseph Polis, Penobscot elder and guide, 1842.

The trip also reminded him that he belonged "part and parcel" to nature, but especially to his hometown. "I shall never find in the wilds of Labrador any greater wildness than in some recess in Concord."

His next great experiment would happen where he had lived most of his life. Could he make a bird-by-bird, flower-by-flower, and leaf-by-leaf guide—a Concord Kalendar—to the natural events of the year?

November 26	November 28	November 30
Watching fish under ice	Neighbor heard wildcat "yow yow yow" near Walden	Air full of geese

Next comes Winter.

Now we see the ground
covered with snow, and
the trees are bare.

Those who questioned Henry's summer rambles after flowers thought treks in winter were downright strange.

But there was as much to discover in glove-weather as in any other. He counted rings on oak stumps to study their growth, and measured how far pine seedlings sprouted from a parent tree.

tree rings

In a bare willow, he found a yellow warbler nest and learned she lined the cup with milkweed silk.

pine seedling

December 1	December 2	December 3
Cut down hickory to count rings	First lesser redpoll	Caught severe cold counting tree rings

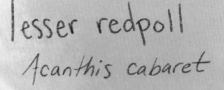

lesser redpoll
Acanthis cabaret

Sometimes he followed a fox's track or skated on the frozen Concord River, just for fun. If only his neighbors would come outside, he could show them wonders. "You shall walk on water, all these brooks and rivers and ponds shall be your highway."

Henry's walking stick — used to measure snow depth

December 4

Wind shaking house

December 5

Birches glazed in ice

Townsfolk would brave the cold for lectures at the Concord Lyceum. Professor Agassiz, Reverend Theodore Parker, and Concord's famous philosopher, Ralph Waldo Emerson, spoke to packed halls.

Henry gave his first Lyceum lecture in April 1838, trying out some journal ideas before turning them into an essay.

CONCORD LYCEUM

Nov. 18, (Introductory) R. W. Emerson, Concord.
"   30, R. W. Emerson, Concord.
Dec. 7, James Richardson, Cambridge.
"   14, James Freeman Clarke, Boston.
"   19, Horace Greeley, N. York.
"   21, Wendell Phillips, Boston.
"   28, O. A. Brownson, Chelsea.
Jan.   4, Clarke Lane, England.
"   11, M. B. Prichard, Concord.
"   18, John B. Keyes, Cambridge.
"   25, J. F. Barrett, Boston.
Feb.   1, C. T. Jackson, "
"   8, H. D. Thoreau, Concord.

shepherd's Purse

Capsella bursa-pastoris

December 7

Warm, shepherd's
purse blooming

By the 1850s, neighbors
looked forward to his talks
on living simply and battling
woodchucks at Walden Pond.
After a lecture on wild apples,
a teacher in town remarked on
how the audience laughed at
the witty talk, "full of juice."

Ralph Waldo Emerson

Few realized then that his most
important talk told about his night
in jail. The weighty title, "The
Rights and Duties of the Individual
in Relation to Government," put off some listeners; the call for
personal sacrifice to protect strangers' rights repelled many others.

Icy walks to Walden felt warmer than his essay's reception.
Thinking of the sharply divided nation, his steps sometimes
dragged. He asked, "what signifies the beauty of nature
when men are base?"

December 8	December 9	December 10
Followed large owl, inclined to think short-eared	Goldenrod withered above snow; river suddenly frozen	Squirrel tracks to walnut trees

Frederick Douglass, autobiography

In the stormiest Decembers, Henry gained strength from the abolitionists—people dedicated to ending slavery. His mother, his sisters, and Abigail May Alcott and Lidian Emerson all joined the Concord Female Anti-Slavery Society. When two churches in town banned speakers they called radicals, the women invited the country's most powerful abolitionist to their own meeting.

December 12	December 14	December 15
First snow buntings	First snow fleas	Last of geese

Frederick Douglass, who had fled from slavery on a
Maryland farm, shared stories of life in that "horrible pit."
Brilliant and fiery, Douglass made his listeners feel his
suffering, and also his joy in seizing freedom at last—not
in the woods, but in New York City. "I felt like one who
had escaped a den of hungry lions."

How could
anyone hear
such mighty
words and not
demand change?

*highbush
blueberry*

December 18
|
*Very cold,
windy*

December 20
|
*Highbush blueberry
leaves still red*

In a Boston church in 1859, 2,500 people gathered to hear Henry. Though many in the crowd opposed him, he steeled himself to speak out for condemned prisoner John Brown.

On October 16, 1859, Brown had led an attack on the federal arsenal at Harper's Ferry, Virginia. The fierce abolitionist was determined to ignite rebellion against slavery. Sixteen people were killed, and the defeated Brown and other surviving raiders were captured by U.S. Marines.

Raid at Harper's Ferry:

Some abolitionists in the audience rejected all violence, even to serve the great cause. Many others in the country scorned Brown as a murderer and dangerously insane.

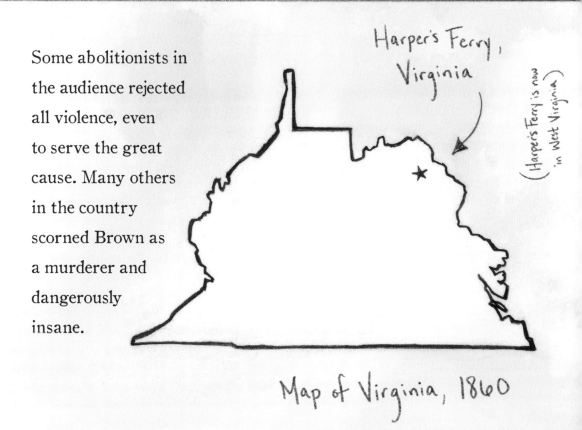

Harper's Ferry, Virginia

(Harper's Ferry is now in West Virginia.)

Map of Virginia, 1860

Henry too detested violence, yet he was among the first to speak in Brown's support. In a voice like a torrent, long remembered in Boston, Henry called Brown a man of principle who offered his life to end injustice. True, few had risen to join the revolt, Henry admitted. But then, "when were the good and the brave ever in the majority?" Henry wanted his audience to wake up as citizens, to wake up and *act.*

December 21	December 22	December 24
Ruddy-colored scarlet oak leaves	Thaw in night	Pine grosbeaks in apple trees

The cold is so intense that the rivers and brooks are frozen.

After a light snow, Henry often strapped on skates to glide down the river. Not a leaf rustled or insect buzzed, and Henry found peace in the crystal silence.

The snowy banks revealed quiet secrets as he passed. Feathers without fox tracks showed where a hawk might have taken a quail. A muskrat chasing fish, glimpsed under ice, hinted at the wild lives he still barely knew.

Northern bobwhite — Colinus virginianus

Snowshoes he'd found
in farmers' attics were
traces of another secret—
Concord winters must have
been colder in decades past. Did Algonquian
people in these woods meet sharper
winds and deeper snows?

Henry's
Snowshoes

muskrat
Ondatra
zibethicus

In 1859, Henry had nearly ten years of detailed notes
about Concord seasons, but no clear answers to his
questions. He kept recording. "The earth is not a
mere fragment of dead history," he wrote, "but living
poetry like the leaves of a tree, which precede flower
and fruit—not a fossil earth but a living earth."

Tensions over slavery mounted across the nation, but on New Year's Day, 1860, Henry encountered a different kind of rebellion. With Bronson Alcott and other local thinkers at a dinner party, he read aloud an advance copy of Charles Darwin's new book, *On the Origin of Species*.

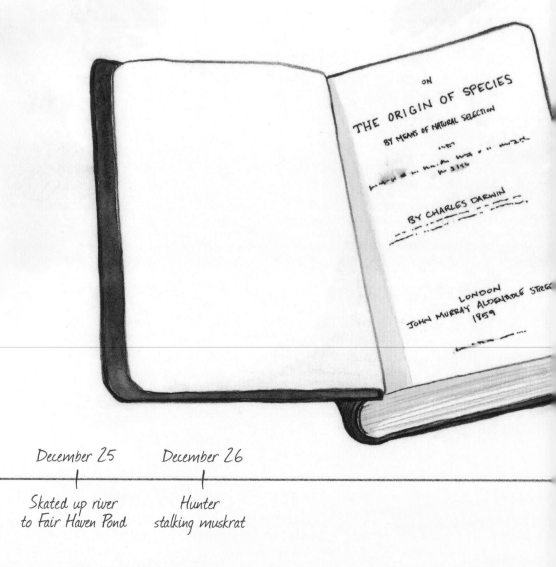

ON
THE ORIGIN OF SPECIES
BY MEANS OF NATURAL SELECTION

BY CHARLES DARWIN

LONDON
JOHN MURRAY ALDEMARLE STREET
1859

December 25

Skated up river
to Fair Haven Pond

December 26

Hunter
stalking muskrat

vesper sparrow
Pooecetes gramineus

The book was already rocking
Victorian society by challenging
the conviction that God had created people and nature to
exist unchanged through eternity. Perhaps more shocking,
Darwin argued that the struggle for life between species
determines survival or extinction and drives creative
change on Earth.

In coming weeks, Henry re-read the book, copying long
passages to remember. He redoubled his studies of trees
and other plants, recognizing a "greater vital force in
nature," "more flexible and accommodating," thanks
to Darwin's intellectual revolution. The new theory had
confirmed a joyful insight in Henry's own *Walden*: "The
universe is wider than our views of it."

December 31	January 1	January 3
Goldfinch eating hemlock	Vesper sparrow flocks	Redpolls feeding on birch catkins

Henry's drawing of a hawk feather

"Winter has a concentrated and nutty kernel if you know where to look for it," said Henry. He would wade miles through deep snow to greet favorite trees just as he kept appointments with old friends.

Reading Darwin's *Origin* renewed Henry's energy for the Kalendar project. By a woodstove, he mined his journal and scraps of field notes for the smallest details about Concord's seasonal events. Just listing years of notes was a monumental task, but then the notes needed to be organized for analysis.

hickory leaves & nuts

January 5

Thin driving snow

On newspaper-sized sheets, carefully ruled into neat columns and rows, he scribbled down thousands of hours of observations for every year from 1851 to 1860. A hacking cough kept him inside often in winter 1861. In his attic chamber, simple as his Walden dwelling, Henry pored over records of spring bird arrivals and summer nests, first blooms and ripe fruits, insect songs, and ice melting and crystallization.

One question burned: what patterns would be revealed when the Kalendar was finished, what cycles within cycles that comprise the abundant whole?

January 7	January 8	January 10	January 11
Only walker in woods	Woodpecker in apple trees	Leaf buds on blueberries	Ice on ragweed

There is nothing to be seen.
We have no birds to cheer
us with their morning song.
We hear only the sound of
the sleigh bells.

snowshoe hare — So cute!

Lepus americanus

(hind)

(front)

hare tracks

January 20 — Not a bird or insect is heard

January 25 — Men ice-fishing at Walden

January 27 — Snowshoe hare in shrub oaks

If Henry had regrets about the tedious paperwork, it was only that he hadn't begun sooner. He wrote, "It will take you half a lifetime to find out where to look for the earliest flower."

As his cough deepened, the family feared he was suffering from the illness that had killed his sister Helen: tuberculosis. Yet Henry never wasted worry on sickness. To him, the mystery of death was another natural event, a passage leading toward renewal. "The passing away of one life," wrote Henry, "is the making room for another."

fox tracks in the snow

As warm in the attic as wool could make him, he felt as eager as ever to sniff skunk cabbage in a spring bog. He knew that everywhere under the snow, seeds were waiting to sprout. "I have great faith in a seed," Henry told anyone discouraged by darkness and cold. "Convince me you have a seed there, and I am prepared to expect wonders."

February 2	February 7	February 12
Tracks of fox hunting mice	Sheets froze stiff in night	Cold jay screams

The first shots of the Civil War rang out on April 12, 1861, and a week later, Concord's forty-man militia marched to join the fray. Henry's friend Louisa May Alcott, by then a writer herself, said, "Everyone is boiling over with excitement." But the war dragged on, and Henry would not live to hear the Emancipation Proclamation, which ended slavery in the rebellious states on September 22, 1862. In his last months, Henry relied on sister Sophia to polish a few essays for publication, and friends and family to bring the latest blooms or news of returning warblers to his sick room. The Kalendar would need to be completed by others. Henry David Thoreau died in the morning, on May 6, 1862.

February 18
No bluebird
song yet

February 19
Snow, mile
after mile

February 24
First
bluebird song

Daguerreotype
by Benjamin D. Maxham
~ 1856 ~

Henry's Concord Kalendar

*"Facts collected by a poet are set
down at last as winged seeds of truth."*
—Thoreau's *Journal*, June 19, 1852

When Henry Thoreau proposed to live alone in the woods at Walden Pond, a friend asked, "What would you do there?"

Henry replied, "Will it not be employment enough to watch the progress of the seasons?"

Those observations became the living heart of Thoreau's masterpiece, *Walden*, and other writings. In Henry's time, the science of phenology—research on the timing of natural events like plant blooms and bird migrations—attracted little interest. Writing is what earned him fame. His essay about going to jail to protest slavery, often called "Civil Disobedience," has inspired Martin Luther King Jr. and millions of others to fight injustice. His ideas about living simply, close to nature, have made him a beloved founder of the environmental movement. But seven hundred pages of Thoreau's phenology records, from 1852 to 1862, were stored away as pointless detail, dry and artless.

In 2003, conservation biologist Richard Primack

wanted to investigate how global climate change was affecting his home state of Massachusetts. Henry's yellowing surveyor papers, with column after column of Concord flowering dates in the 1850s, became the foundation for an important investigation.

Dr. Primack and colleagues began to retrace Henry's footsteps around Concord, seeking the plants he had studied to catch their first blooms again. Sadly, about a quarter of the native flowers Henry had admired were gone. The ecologists kept looking, though, and found enough plants to make their own records of blooming and leaf-out, and also noted spring bird arrival dates—on computer spreadsheets—to compare with Henry's 150-year-old observations.

After ten years of compilation and analysis, the datasets began to reveal startling changes around Concord since the 1850s. For example, highbush blueberry bushes and apple trees may flower four weeks earlier than Henry would have expected. Most birds studied still reach Massachusetts around the same date, but yellow warblers and a few others arrive earlier. On average, in 2013, trees and shrubs around Concord were leafing out about two weeks earlier than in Thoreau's day. These are major shifts that have occurred in a blink of geological time.

Much remains to be discovered from this comparative research. How will early blooming and leafing affect plants' health and ability to make seeds? When trees leaf out early, will they shade out forest wildflowers? Will wild animals that depend on each plant adapt to the changes, or will their relationships weaken or break? As temperatures keep rising, which plants will be able to adapt, and which will die off? In an interconnected ecological community, one change can disrupt many parts of a complex web, unraveling connections that have evolved over eons.

The first step toward answering these questions is to gather more information. If each of us becomes a citizen scientist, observing the plants, birds, insects, and other wildlife around us every day, the data we collect will help us understand the natural world—and protect it.

Henry did not have time to finish his Concord Kalendar, but thanks to its rediscovery and to growing numbers of phenologists, ecologists, educators, and community naturalists, "facts collected by a poet are set down at last as winged seeds of truth."

Thoreau and Climate Change

Henry David Thoreau observed for himself that climate varies over time. To study seasons through history, he gathered stories from family and neighbors who remembered New England winters in the past. His mother recalled summer frosts in 1816 that ruined crops on the family farm and in parts of Europe. Scientists later determined that debris from a colossal volcanic eruption had cooled the atmosphere and caused "the year without a summer."

Grooves on rocky Massachusetts hilltops also confirmed Louis Agassiz's 1830s theory that ice sheets had once covered much of the Earth. Later geologists would discover that several great Ice Ages have shaped the planet as we know it. Signs of natural climate change strengthened Thoreau's faith that the Earth is alive, a dynamic system of infinite interest and beauty.

Climatologists today know that human activities can also drive climate shifts. Deforestation, livestock production, draining peatlands, and, especially, the burning of coal, oil, methane gas, and other carbon-based fuels are responsible for raising Earth's average temperature more than 1° Celsius since Thoreau's time.

In the 1850s, when Henry was gathering phenology data, amateur chemist Eunice Foote tested how sunlight affected different gases. She found that carbon dioxide traps heat, and she hypothesized that an atmosphere with more CO_2 would heat the planet. But like Thoreau's seasonal observations, Foote's experiments were largely ignored.

Today, climate change evidence is inescapable. Polar ice is melting, wildfires burn hotter and longer, cities flood on sunny days from rising seas, and coral reefs are dying from underwater heat waves. Wildlife, plants, and people—especially poor and vulnerable people—are at risk. Henry, who measured everything, would shake his head at those who still doubt the facts. And to those who want to find answers quickly, he might now say, "If time is short then you have no time to waste."

A Kalendar of Your Own

"No one, to my knowledge, has observed the minute differences in the seasons. Hardly two nights are alike . . . . A book of the seasons, each page of which should be written in its own season and out-of-doors, or in its own locality wherever it may be."
—Thoreau's *Journal*, June 11, 1852

"The scale on which his studies proceeded was so large as to require longevity, and we were the less prepared for his sudden disappearance. The country knows not yet, or in the least part, how great a son it has lost. It seems an injury that he should leave in the midst his broken task . . . ."
—from Ralph Waldo Emerson's eulogy for Thoreau, expanded in *The Atlantic Monthly*, August 1862

Careful notetaking gave Henry records of his observations over many years. Though he died before he could finish analyzing his data, charting the day-by-day, year-by-year notes confirmed that seasonal changes are more complex and varied than the spring, summer, fall, winter patterns he had learned about in school.

Many factors—cold snaps, heat waves, hurricanes, and

dry spells—can shift the usual timing of blooming and other seasonal events. Even more powerfully, the global climate is getting warmer, causing higher temperatures, heavier rains, droughts, and other major changes. How does the natural world respond to unexpected and shifting conditions?

It takes dedicated work to begin answering this profound question. Each of us can help! Starting a nature calendar is as easy as heading outside with a pencil and notebook. Make notes about the first dandelion or bumblebee you spot in the spring, or the first maple leaf turning red in the fall.

Return to the same place over and over. Follow the life of one plant from first sprout to bud, to bloom, to seed formation and release. To learn more, take along tools such as a magnifying lens to check wildflowers for pollen, or a ruler to measure the caterpillars growing on milkweed. Cellphone apps such as eBird and iNaturalist make recording nature data and sharing it with others easier than ever. Other tools—such as cameras and drawing pencils—add value and fun to data collecting.

Communicate your results with others at science fairs and through citizen-science research projects. Whether you're investigating plants, birds, or other organisms, you'll find a study online where your observations can boost everyone's understanding. It may become part of a published paper or support a management plan to protect a park.

Already, phenologists have evidence of early blooming and egg hatching, shortened hibernations, and other indicators of a changing climate. Some plants and animals appear extra-sensitive to rising temperatures, while others seem more able to adapt. The findings spark new questions: What if a wildflower blooms early but the bees that would pollinate it still follow their historic timing? What will the mice eat that once depended on finding plenty of those seeds? With ancient, intricate relationships at risk, some call the disconnected results "global weirding."

The potential effects of climate change are a vast and complex puzzle. We can help put it together by becoming citizen scientists studying phenology. We can carry on Henry Thoreau's broken task by going outside to build our own books of the seasons.

Resources

Nature Journaling

Leslie, Clare Walker and Charles E. Roth. 2000. *Keeping a Nature Journal.* Storey Publishing.

Wheelwright, Nathaniel T. and Bernd Heinrich. 2017. *The Naturalist's Notebook.* Storey Publishing.

Thoreau Biographies

Smith, Corinne Hosfield. 2016. *Henry David Thoreau for Kids: His Life and Ideas, with 21 Activities.* Chicago Review Press.

Walls, Laura Dassow. 2017. *Thoreau: A Life.* University of Chicago Press.

Wood, David F. 2006. *An Observant Eye.* Concord Museum.

Phenology

Ellwood, Elizabeth R., Richard B. Primack, and Michele L. Talmadge. 2010. Effects of Climate Change on Spring Arrival Times of Birds in Thoreau's Concord from 1851 to 2007. *The Condor* 112(4): 754-762. https://doi.org/10.1525/cond.2010.100006

Hineline, Mark L. 2018. *Ground Truth: A Guide to Tracking Climate Change at Home.* University of Chicago Press.

Miller-Rushing, Abraham and Richard B. Primack. 2008. Global warming and flowering times in Thoreau's Concord: A community perspective. *Ecology* 89(2): 332-41. https://doi.org/10.1890/07-0068.1

Primack, Richard B. 2014. *Walden Warming: Climate Change Comes to Thoreau's Woods.* University of Chicago Press.

Climate Change

Davenport, Leslie. 2021. *All the Feelings Under the Sun: How to Deal with Climate Change.* Magination Press.

Extinction Rebellion. 2019. *This Is Not a Drill.* Penguin Press.

Herbert, Megan and Michael E. Mann. 2022. *The Tantrum that Saved the World.* North Atlantic Books.

Thunberg, Greta. 2019. *No One Is Too Small to Make a Difference.* Penguin Classics.

Websites

Budburst is a community science project that collects phenology data to improve plant conservation. https://budburst.org

Journey North is a leading citizen science project that maps data collected throughout North America for science and conservation education. https://journeynorth.org

The Thoreau Farm protects Thoreau's birth house and carries forward his insights into nature, humanity, and social responsibility. https://thoreaufarm.org/thoreau-birth-house

Thoreau's Kalendar is a digital archive of Thoreau's phenological records. https://thoreauskalendar.org/about.html

USA National Phenology Network brings together students, educators, scientists, and organizations to study how climate change is impacting plants and animals in the U.S. https://www.usanpn.org

The Walden Woods Project works to protect the land and further the legacy of Henry David Thoreau. https://www.walden.org

Data Collection Apps

eBird records bird sightings for personal, recreational, and scientific uses including National Audubon's Climate Watch study of how climate change is affecting wild birds. https://ebird.org

iNaturalist makes it easy to collect and share plant and animal observations for biodiversity studies. https://www.inaturalist.org

Seek is a virtual plant field guide, using visual recognition software to identify species. https://www.inaturalist.org/pages/seek_app

To Jasper. "Surely joy is the condition of life." —J.D.

Julie Dunlap is an award-winning children's writer whose books include *Louisa May and Mr. Thoreau's Flute; Parks for the People; Extraordinary Horseshoe Crabs*; and *John Muir and Stickeen*. Her edited anthologies for adult readers include *Coming of Age at the End of Nature: A Generation Faces Living on a Changed Planet*. She teaches wildlife ecology and environmental studies at the University of Maryland Global Campus.

For Jeremy, my loving husband. —M.E.B.

Megan Elizabeth Baratta is a children's book illustrator living in upstate New York with her husband and a cat named Pip. She loves rendering scenes of ordinary life and showing their quiet beauty, as in her picture book *Most Days* (Tilbury House, 2021). You can visit her at www.barattastudio.com.

"Live in each season as it passes—breathe the air, drink the drink,
taste the fruit, & resign yourself to the influences of each."
—Thoreau's *Journal*, August 23, 1853

Text © 2022 by Julie Dunlap • Illustrations © 2022 by Megan Elizabeth Baratta
Hardcover ISBN 978-0-88448-908-5 • 10 9 8 7 6 5 4 3 2
Library of Congress Control Number: 2021948053

Tilbury House Publishers • Thomaston, Maine • www.tilburyhouse.com
Designed by Frame25 Productions • Printed in China

Excerpts from the childhood essay "The Seasons," by David Henry Thoreau (who later became Henry
David), are taken from p.27 of *The Days of Henry Thoreau*, by Walter Harding (Knopf, 1965), based
on a copy of the original Thoreau manuscript in the Special Collections, Concord Free Public Library.

Historical Image Credits

page 4: Samuel W. Rowse crayon portrait of Thoreau 1854, courtesy of Special Collections, Concord Free Public Library • p.4:
facsimile of 1906 map by Herbert W. Gleason showing places mentioned in Thoreau's *Journals*, courtesy of Special Collections,
Concord Free Public Library • p.12: Louis Agassiz photo from the *New York Public Library Digital Collections* • p.20: Thoreau's
survey of Walden Pond, courtesy of Special Collections, Concord Free Public Library • p.24: front cover of the first issue of *The
Dial*, courtesy of the Walden Woods Project • p.30: Thoreau's Walden Pond house as drawn by his sister Sophia, from *Walden*
(1854) • p.48: photograph of Sophia Thoreau, courtesy of Special Collections, Concord Free Public Library • p.48: 1851 broadside
in response to the Fugitive Slave Act of 1850, courtesy Library of Congress • p.49: photograph of Helen Thoreau, courtesy of
Special Collections, Concord Free Public Library • p.52: Thoreau's survey map of the Alcott estate, courtesy of Special Collections,
Concord Free Public Library • pp.54-55: Concord town center, by John Warner Barber, from *Historical collections: being a general
collection of interesting facts, traditions, biographical sketches, anecdotes, &c., relating to the history and antiquities of every town in
Massachusetts: with geographical descriptions* (Dorr, Howland & Co., Worcester, 1839, p. 377) • p.60: 1854 sketch of Thoreau in
greatcoat, from *Daniel Ricketson and His Friends* (1902) • p.63: 1842 portrait of Joseph Polis by Charles
Bird King, courtesy Gilcrease Museum, Tulsa, OK • p.69: photo of Ralph Waldo Emerson ca.
1857, from commons.wikimedia • p.70: title page *Narrative of the Life of Frederick Douglass,
an American Slave*, 1847, accessed at https://archive.org/details/douglasfred00dougrich
• p.72: the 1859 raid at Harper's Ferry, courtesy Library of Congress • p.78: drawing
of hawk feather from Thoreau's *Journal*, 11/11/1858 (1906 edition), courtesy of the
Walden Woods Project • p.79: page of Thoreau's bird observations, 1851-54, from the
Ernst Mayr Library and Archives of the Museum of Comparative Zoology, Harvard
University • p.83: 1856 daguerreotype of Thoreau, courtesy of the National Portrait
Gallery, Smithsonian Institution